THE BELLS

OF THE

CATHEDRAL CHURCH

OF

S. PETER, EXON,

BY

HENRY THOMAS ELLACOMBE, M.A., F.S.A.

EXETER:
PRINTED FOR THE AUTHOR BY WILLIAM POLLARD, NORTH STREET.
1874.

In the interest of creating a more extensive selection of rare historical book reprints, we have chosen to reproduce this title even though it may possibly have occasional imperfections such as missing and blurred pages, missing text, poor pictures, markings, dark backgrounds and other reproduction issues beyond our control. Because this work is culturally important, we have made it available as a part of our commitment to protecting, preserving and promoting the world's literature. Thank you for your understanding.

PREFACE.

The following account of the Bells of the Cathedral was first printed in the Transactions of the Exeter Diocesan Architectural Society, but in scattered and irregular portions: they are now brought together in regular order, and in a form which will be more convenient for the general reader.

H. T. E.

S. Peter's Day, 1874.

THE BELLS OF THE CATHEDRAL CHURCH OF S. PETER, EXON.

As a Ring of Ten the heaviest in Metal, and grandest in Tone in the whole World.

It may be gathered from the Fabric Rolls, examined by Dr. Oliver, from 1286 to 1439, which, by the kind permission of the Dean and Chapter I have also been allowed to see, that there were at that early period ten bells. Such an unusual number can only be accounted for by supposing that some of them were provided for certain services, and were hung within the choir or nave, as it appears by Rocca, in his *Treatise on Bells* (1612), and Carlo Borromeo, that seven was the number allowed to a Cathedral tower.[1]

These names appear on the Rolls:

1286 *Walter*, (for jobs, 2^s) called from the donor, Bishop Walter Bronescombe.

Bockerel, hanging,—. } in the North Tower, with two others.
Chauncel, hanging,—.

Germacyn, (Qy.) from Ralph Germacyn, Precentor, 1308 to 1316. 2^d

1319 *Jesus*, 2^s 6^d ironwork.   In St. John's, or South Tower.
1323 *St. Mary*, repairs, 11^d.   In St. Paul's, or North Tower.

---

[1] Bishop Leofric, 1050, found seven bells in the Cathedral: he is recorded to have added six others and a dozen smaller ones, probably for chimes. In Dugdale's Monasticon, vol. ii., p. 527, Ed: 1817, this passage occurs in the Latin version of a Saxon M.S. in the Bodleian Library, auct. D. 2.16, fol. 1 *a*: "Erant autem antea nisi septem campanæ suspensæ, nunc sunt tredecim suspensæ, præter duodecim tintinnabula."

1351 *Peter*,[1] —6ᶜ· "The Base."[2] "*De novo facta*" in 1330.
1372 One of the bells was cast or recast.
1396 *Trinity*, repairs. —
1396 *Grandison*, in the North Tower with three others, repairs, 12ᵈ·
1399 For repairing the four bells in the North Tower, 15ᵈ·
1415 *Bracton*, repairs, 14ᵈ·
1452-3, is a charge of xxᵈ· "*in una bauderick pro maxima campana in campanile borcali.*"

Of the bells here enumerated, there are only two at present known by the same name: viz., *Grandison*, which is the Tenor of the ring of ten, and *Great Peter;* but *that* Peter must have been different from the present one, which was the gift of Bishop Courtenay in 1484.

There is a tradition at Llandaff, that our Peter bell was taken from that city in exchange for five bells brought from Exeter, in Bishop Courtenay's time; and certain it is, that the tower of Llandaff was built 1484, the date of the gift of this bell.[3]

There is another tradition that Cardinal Wolsey about 1513, when Lord High Chancellor, and possessed of the revenues of the Bishopric of Tournay, sent over from that place five large bells, and distributed them to divers Cathedrals; the smallest he gave to Sherborne, (that he gave one there is no doubt, as it was inscribed) and one to Exeter.[4] Be that as it may, it is perhaps hopeless now to find out the true history of the whole of the original bells of our Cathedral, nor how they were broken or destroyed.

However, I have been successful in finding the name of the founder of the bells set up in Bishop Quivil's time, and I believe he will turn out to be the earliest one of his craft known in the kingdom.

---

[1] Probably so called from Bishop Peter Quivil.

[2] A term not known at present; it probably means the *biggest bell*.

[3] Dr. Oliver (*History of Exeter*, p. 64) remarks, "that, although the date 1453 was twenty-five years before Courtenay was made Bishop, yet precisely in that year he was appointed Archdeacon of Exeter; and perhaps on that occasion may have offered such valuable presents."

[4] Strype's *Annals* and Hutchins' *Dorset*.

By the kindness of the principal officers in our Public Record Office in London, I am enabled to publish, for the first time, the name of Roger de Ropeforde *(Campanistarius)*, of Paignton, whose son William, and grandson Robert, as next heir, carried on the business at the close of the thirteenth and beginning of the fourteenth centuries, and were the parties employed by Bishop Quivil and the Chapter in 1284 to make the four bells in the North Tower, which we find recited in the Fabric Rolls just quoted. They were also engaged to repair the organs and the horologe.

In an Inspeximus Charter of Edward II (*Patent Roll*, Part i, *m.* 5.) is a recital of a deed of Bishop Quivil, dated ij Ides of July, 1284, by which he grants a tenement, with house and land at Paignton, to Roger de Ropeford, his son and heirs, for the annual payment of one penny at Easter, in consideration of which they are to make the bells for the Cathedral, and repair the organs and horologe, the Chapter, who were consenting parties, undertaking to provide all things necessary for the work to be done; also victuals and drink whenever they are so employed. From not having examined the original Record, both Dr. Oliver in his *Lives of the Bishops of Exeter* (p. 178), and Britton in his *History of the Cathedral* (p. 123), were misled by an erroneous entry in the published Calendar of the Patent Rolls, which gives the name of "Robert son of Walter" only, and that he was to toll the bells, whereas the Record is a confirmation to Robert, the grandson of Roger de Ropeford, of the same premises in Paignton, for the same services and payment by which they were first granted by the Bishop. (See the Record at the end.)

In the Fabric Roll 1285, is the entry of the following payments to them.

"Item in ferramento Campane que vocatur *clermatyn* ij^d.

"Item in rotacione.........Campanarum xij^d.

"Itm Rogero Campanistario et filio ejus ad pendendum duas Campanas scilicet *Cokerel* et *Chaunterel* ij^s.

"Fabro pro ferro et opere ad ferramenta earundam v^s."

How long they enjoyed this privilege does not appear, but from entries in the Fabric Rolls, 1372—3, in Bishop Brantingham's time, they were no longer employed by the Capitular Body, for other persons were engaged in casting two bells, the details of the cost are set forth in the following extract:

"Compotus Domini Willielmi Trendlebeare custodis operis beati Petri Exoniensis.

"Custus campane ad clokk. mccclxxii.—mccclxxiii.

"In stipendio Laurentii Drake xij^d; Ricardi Slade x^d; et Johannis Cobleigh x^d; circa fusum cadum et formam campane, et Ricardi Hope ad ligandum prædictum vj^d

"In cariagio bituminis et bitumine emto vj^s

"In stipendio Johannis Brown, Roberti Facy, circa fornacem per iiij dies iij^s iiij^d; et Ricardi Drebel per tres dies xiij$\frac{1}{2}^d$

"In cc bordnayls xj^d; et in xvi spykys ij^d; in feno empto pro fornace iij^d; in stipendio Ricardi Drebel plaustrantis prædictam fornacem ij^s ij$\frac{1}{2}^d$; in una libra cere empta pro literis campane viij^d; in xxiij libris pinguedinis boum ij^s vj^d; in canabo et in filo canabo empto xix^d; in ligacione cape campane cum ligno xiij^d ob; in stipendio Ricardi Drebel ad fodiendum puteum pro campana xx^d; et in uno summo straminis empto vii^d

"*Summa* xxv^s v^d

"*Empcio metalli*. In xxxv libris cupri emptis a Johanne Brasyer de Dertemouthe xxvj£ xiij^s iv^d precium libre iij$\frac{1}{2}^d$; In vj^c xvi libris stagni Willielmo Ryka de Ayschperton emptis v£ ij^s x^d precium libre ij^d; in cariagio xij^d; et in ij^c xxxij libris metalli emptis in diversis locis lvij^s ij^d·

"*Summa* xxxiij£ xiv^s iv^d

"In carbonetis emptis xv^s iij^d; in uno quarterio carbonetis lapidis empto iv^s; in duobus summis focalis de Stokwode iij$\frac{1}{2}^d$; in expensis in purificatione metalli et fusione campane xiij^s; et in follibus conductis ad id complendam ij^s

"*Summa* xxxiij^s vij$\frac{1}{2}^d$

"In solucione facta *Thome Karoun* alias Belhutero pro labore suo x£ xix^s

"In expensis suis versus Dertemouthe iij^s et ex præcepto dominorum meorum xij^d

"In solucione facta Nicholao Bealde ad adjuvandum prædictum Thomam in opere prædicto per xix septimanas xij^s

"*Summa* xj£ xv^s

"Custus alterius campane.

"In cariagio butuminis xxj^d; in pinguedine boum xix^{li} iij^s vij^d; in cera empta pro literis iiij^d; in uno homine conducto ad superintendendam formam campane per ij dies ix^d; in pinguedine porcorum et schynzina vj^d; in canabo et in filo canabi ij^s ij^d; in una plata empta iiij^d; in ligacione cape cum ligno iiij^d; et cum ferro de proprio vj^s; et in quatuor summis focalis de Stokwode vj^d ob; in uno summo straminis vj^d; et in stipendio Ricardi Drebel locato ad fodiendum puteum pro campana per ij dies et dimidiam x^d; et in una stapela pro campana viij^d; et in solucione facta Thome Karoun alias Belhutero iij^{li} vi^s viij^d.

"*Summa* iiij^{li} iiij^s xj^d ob.

* * * * * *

"Item, in solucione Gulielmo Crockarneville pro cruce campanilis et Johanni Snel cum toto apparatu ad exaltandam campanam integram xxx^s x^d; in emendacione unius clapere de Graunson iiij^d"

* * * * * *

These may certainly be considered among the very earliest records relating to the casting of bells. Aware of their great interest when I first found them in the Fabric Rolls—which, by the courteous permission of the late Dean, I was allowed to examine—circumstances prevented my taking a copy at that time, and I depended upon getting the whole entry photographed; but as there was some difficulty about that, my friend, the late Mr. Barnes, kindly promised to make an exact copy and took charge of the Roll for that purpose; but other more serious matters engrossed his attention, and it was never done till Mr. Stewart Moore's attention was lately called to it.

We now come to September 29, 1339, the date of Bishop Grandisson's *Statutes* for the government of his Collegiate Establishment at Ottery St. Mary (No. 15), the number and position of the bells in each tower are given, and how, and on what occasions they were to be sounded.

15. "Item statuimus quod omni die per annum extra feriam sextam parasceves[1] et sabbato sancto cantetur solempnis missa de beata Maria in capella ejusdem atequam pulsetur ad primam diei; ad quam missam in omnibus majoribus duplicibus festis per totum annum maxima campana ecclesie pulsetur; in mediis vero duplicibus secunda major campana: in omnibus aliis duplicibus tercia major campana: et quando 'Invitatorium' tercio habetur, quarta major: et predicte quatuor majores campane debeant pendere sicut Exonie in parte ecclesie dextra, et alie cotidie quatuor in sinistra, quarum majores semper ad missam beate Marie pulsetur nisi in predictis temporibus, et semper cum illa campana que debet pulsari ad missam beate Marie, pulsari debet Ignitegium. Pulsabitur ad missam sic: Primo illa campana, cum qua pulsari debet, terminatur octo vel decem ictibus continuis, et facto bono intervallo quasi dimidii miliarii[2] pulsetur cum eadem campana per dimidium miliarii et cessetur et iterum statim repulsetur eadem per totum tempus, ut primo, et cessetur; et statim tercia pulsetur brevius; et tunc celeriter clerici omnes et pueri cum duobus ad minus, vicariis, vadant sine mora ad capellam beate Marie, et dictis horis beate Marie, cum sufficiens numerus venerit, incipiatur statim missa et terminetur campana."

[1] Good Friday.

[2] I have submitted this difficult phrase to some high classical scholars, who are of opinion that the meaning is *half of a thousand*, and that the passage should be construed in this way—"after a good interval, say whilst you could count 500" (which would be about three minutes), "let the same bell be tolled," &c. The adjective "miliarius" was often used in the same kind of way in more classical Latin, with the word "spatium" or "numerous" understood. Or "miliarium" may be taken as a substantive, and "dimidius" as the neuter of the adjective "dimidius," and then it would be at the interval of "about a thousand halved," which would bring it to the same thing. It is difficult to understand how the late Dr. Oliver (Monas. Exon., p. 269) could construe it " Rung with a half-wheel, or dead rope!"

The Rev. E. C. Walcott suggests the following explanation: I believe this means simply " with the protraction of half-a-mile,"—the bell ringing for the time in which one of the vicars could walk the distance, being "in villa;" so by the statutes of York, 1294, they rang for Matins, whilst our Lady Matins were being sung, and for Prime whilst a man could walk the three miles from Loughtenton to York.

We may also call attention to his directions for sounding the bells at funerals, though his reason for inhibiting long ringings ("Sicut Exonie") are very remarkable—looking at the date, 1339, viz., "that they do no good to the departed, are an annoyance to the living, and injurious to the fabrick and the bells."[1]

The next records relating to the Bells are in a beautifully written Leger Book among the archives of the Cathedral of uncertain date,[2] probably in Bishop Brantingham's time: it may be the volume named by Dugdale[3] as being one of the MSS. in the possession of the Dean and Chapter, though it has no title.

De pulsatione[4] Campanarum in Ecclesia Exoniensi et modo pulsationis singulis diebus per annum.

In majoribus duplicibus[5] festis[6] utreque vespere[7] et matutine[8] in pulsatione consonant. Primo enim due mediocres, secundo due magne,

---

[1] Sec. 76: "Insuper statuimus quod Classicum pulsetur pro mortuis par cum antequam incipitur ' Placebo,' quousque inchoeter ' Dirige,' et similiter ante missam dum dicuntur Commendaciones. Ita, videlicet, quod tam in obitibus quam eciam quando corpus presens habetur secundum dignitatem persone brevius vel longius predictis semper temporibus pulsetur cum majoribus et pluribus vel minoribns et paucioribus campanis; sed inhibemus ne nimis prolixe pulsentur, nec iterum post officium vel in aurora; sicut solet Exonie; quia nichil prodest animabus ' æs sonans aut cymbalum tinniens,' et tamen multum nocet auribus et fabrice ac campanis."

[2] M.S. penes, Dec. et Cap. Exon. No. 3625, fo. 102:

[3] Statuta et Consuetudines Ecclesiæ Exon: cum Calendario veteri, fol.—Dugdale, vol. ij., p. 252. Edit. 1819.

[4] *Pulsatio—pulsare signa.—Campanas*, the French expression "Sonner les Cloches."—Sonner which means tolling, or tingling them, as a house bell is sounded. In Mediæval times, Bells could not be rung up, as they were not hung with whole wheels: so that Pulsatio means simply sounding or tolling, or "*knollyng*," the very word used in a Clause Roll, 9 Henry V. (A D. 1421), No. 31, relating to a dispute between the Prior and citizens of Bath, about the time *pulsare campanas*.

"The ringing for the seven Canonical Hours in large Churches where the custom was followed, (as we here see it was at Exeter), let the world know the time by day and by night: and the several bells, and the different ways in which they were rung for the purpose, told that precise Service which was then about to be chanted."—*Roch*, v. iij., p. 143.

[5] Double or more solemn Services in singings, vestments, &c., &c.

[6] Solemn days dedicated to the memory of some Saint.

[7] *Vespers*, the evensong service at 6 p.m.

[8] *Matins and Lauds*, the Service in the early hours between midnight and prime.

tertio due majores si habeantur, et quarto simul omnes campane ad classicum[1] sunt pulsande. Sunt tamen quedam festa privilegiata que habent ad initium primi sonitus matutinarum quoddam magnum classicum—*e.g.* magnum quarto, videlicet—primus dies Natalis—primus dies Pasche—dies Apostolorum Petri et Pauli—et dies Assumptionis beate Virginis. Ad utramque vero[2] nonam et utrumque completorium[3] ad Te Deum—et ad primam[4] ad processionem[5]—et ad sequentiam[6] pulsantur simul due de majoribus. Sed ad completorium pulsatur quamdiu cantatur usque ad Kyrie eleyson et sic finitur sonitus. Te Deum similiter usque ad versum *per singulos dies,* &c., tunc adjungitur classicum omnium campanarum usque ad initium laudum. Ad processionem vero et ad sequentiam quamdiu durant. Ad terciam[7] pulsatur una de magnis, et ad initium misse classicum, et similiter ad *Ite missa est*; aliud. Sexta[8] vero non habet aliquo tempore alteram pulsationem quando sequitur missam, nisi illam que fit dicta missa sine classico. Sed ad priman quo facto primo sonitu duplo—post aliquantulam pausationem pulsatur iterum cum uno signo ad clericos convocandos, ante priman: pulsatur unum de minoribus signis quod vocant *altisonum,*[9] quo advocant seniores: et idem sonitus post primam, ad capitulum et similiter fit ante completorium.

De pulsatione in Minoribus[10] duplicibus Festis.

In minoribus duplicibus pulsatur fere simili modo sicut in majoribus non privilegiatis:—Paucis exceptis, scilicet quod vespere et matutine primo tamen duabus minoribus—secundo cum duabus mediocribus—tertio cum duabus magnis pulsantur campanis In classicis enim et omnibus aliis concordant cum majoribus que processionibus carent.

[1] *Classicum,* is "pulsatio omnium Campanarum," or sounding them in succession. We cannot suppose they would sound all the bells at the same moment, which would be clashing.

[2] Nona, the ninth hour, 3 p.m.   [3] Compline, the closing or last Service of the day, 8 p.m.

[4] Prime, the first daily Service at 6 a.m.

[5] A procession of persons from the Sanctuary to the choir, or from the choir round the Church inside or outside.

[6] A Song of Exultation, or Jubilation, so called from being chanted after the Gradual.

[7] Tierce, or Undern, Mass at 9 a.m.   [8] Sexts, Service at Noon.

[9] The Treble.   [10] Not so full as the Double Service.

De modo pulsationis in communibus et simplicibus Festis.

In communibus et simplicibus festis eq pulsatur per omnia, videlicet prima nona cum magno signo : vespere et matutine primo cum parvo—secundo cum majori—tertio cum duabus—quarto cum omnibus, absque magnis. Per singulos dies ante Laudem et ad initium misse classicum quale ad vesperas et ad matutinas. Ad primam tertiam et ultimam nonam et utrumque completorium pulsatur cum uno de mediocribus : prima quoque et tertia et completorium—*altisonum* habent sicut duplicia. Sequentia vero pulsatur cum duobus mediocribus quotiescumque dicitur sequentia tam in festis quam pro-festis Ex^{alij} festa duplicia similiter cum uno ejusdem generis paululum post missam. Sed diebus quibus sexta dicenda est ante missam pulsatur sicut ad tertiam et hoc tam in festis quam pro-festis.

De modo pulsationis tam in pro-festis diebus quam feriatis.[1]

In omnibus aliis diebus tam festis quam feriis per totum annum vespere et matutine, pulsantur primo—cum uno de minoribus—secundo cum minori de mediocribus—testio cum majori ejusdemmodi—quarto cum eisdem duabus copulatis. Ante laudes pulsatur cum uno de mediocribus similiter ad tertiam et utramque nonam. Prima vero et completorium sicut ad primum sonitum vesperarum et matutinarum pulsatur—sed completorium non pulsatur nisi circa solis occasum propter operarios, licet tunc non cantetur: post vesperas enim statim cantatur absque intervallo. In talibus diebus tertia habet *altisonum.* Ad capitulum pulsatur cum eodem quo et prima.

De modo pulsationis ad processiones per totum annum, que fiunt tam in ecclesia quam extra ut in rogationibus contra Regem, Archiepiscopum, Episcopum, et alias hujusmodi personas que cum processione deberent recipi, et contra mortuos.

Nota etiam, quod ad processiones pulsatur hoc modo, primo cum

---

[1] Week days, without any particular Office.

mediocri—secundo cum majori ejusdem generis—tertio cum grosso[1] et sic deinceps ascendendo usque ad quintum sonum. Similiter fit per totum annum in majoribus et minoribus festis cujuscumque dignitatis, dominicis et aliis, si placuerit pulsatoribus—quandoque tamen sonat unum grossum ter pro tribus, et hoc in simplicibus dominicis et inferioribus. In omnibus duplicibus pulsatur dupliciter cum magnis signis quandiu processio durat. In simplicibus vero non dominicis pulsantur duo mediocres in introitu chori. In rogationibus et talibus processionibus que fiunt extra ecclesiam pro aliqua necessitate in redeundo in ingressu circuitorii pulsatur classicum particulare. Sed in vigilia Ascensionis Domini generale cum omnibus signis in hujusmodi enim diebus, non pulsatur aliter ad nonam nisi per hujuscemodi classica. Si vero venerit Rex aut Archiepiscopus, aut Episcopus vel alia talis persona que cum processione debet recipi, pulsantur duo magna signa ab illa hora qua suburbio visus vel denunciatus est appropinquare, quousque in ecclesiam personaliter introducatur. Cum vero processio fit contra mortuos pulsatur classicum ex quo cimiterium ingrediuntur venientes cum funere quousque in chorum intrat clerus, et simul ad processionem post missam. Et quo chorum exeunt quousque sepeliatur corpus.

De Classico pulsando contra Corpus Episcopi Decani Canonici Vicarii et in Anniversariis eorundem.

Classica pro mortuis hoc modo fiunt: Cum Episcopus ecclesie aut Decanus mortuus fuerit, statim pulsari debent tria classica pro eo quacumque hora diei hoc denunciatum fuerit, cum universis signis, hoc modo: uno et eodem ictu, et subito simul omnes incipiant pulsare, et aliquandiu pulsationem continuent—et terminato classico, due mediocres campane sine cessatione sonent dum alie pausant. Iterum fiat classicum ut prius, et denuo continuata media pulsatione tercium, et sic finiatur.

---

[1] Query "*the Base,*" repaired 1330 (see p. 2), or "*the third thick bell,*" ordered to be recast by Mr. Pennington, April 1625 (which see).

Similiter fit in obitu cujuslibet Canonici excepto eo quod media pulsatio fit cum duobus de minoribus signis. Quando vero Corpus Episcopi Decani vel Canonici de domo sua ad ecclesiam defertur, semper ab exitu domus ejus continue pulsetur classicum quousque in chorum ecclesie perducatur. Simili modo fit in crastino, dum ejus commendatio dicitur ab inceptione—psalmi " *Legem pone*"[1] usque ad finem commendationis. Similiter quoque fit post missam ab ea hora qua Corpus elevatur ut ad tumulum deferatur, quousque sepulture compleatur officium. In Anniversariis vero aliorum fiunt classica cum omnibus minoribus, et uno magno, nisi sint aliqui quibus fit aliqua specialis gratia et exceptis illis qui habent solempne officium—ut Rex Athelstanus, Decanus Serlo,[2] Archidiaconus Symon,[3] Ysaac,[4] Eustachius[5] et alii secundum quod in Martilogio continetur.[6] In Anniversariis Episcoporum ecclesie classica fiunt cum omnibus signis et ad vesperas et ad commendationem. In exequiis Vicariorum defunctorum post vesperas, chorus vadit et interim pulsatur classicum cum omnibus signis. Similiter in crastino ad receptionem corporis ante missam et post missam ad tumulationem, cum omnibus quidem aliis dispensatur secundum gradus et dignitates tam clericis quam laicis. Ita semper quod inter primam et tertiam tantum pulsatur classicum pro illis, et quod post completorium non pulsetur nec ante vesperas nisi pro predictis personis, et nisi in casu pro aliquo magno transeunte. Hoc enim, si voluntas Decani et Capituli affuerit fieri potest qualibet hora diei. Pro Episcopis vero et Regibus, quia major missa pro eis celebratur, inter tertiam et sextam fit eorum commendatio et classicum cum ea ut supradictum est. Pro famulis Canonicorum fiunt classica, sed non adeo magna, scilicet cum tot signis sicut pro ipsis Canonicis.

Et nota, duod in classicis pro mortuis, ante eorum susceptiones fieri

---

[1] Psalm cxix., v. 33.
[2] The first Dean; he died 1231.
[3] Archdeacon of Cornwall about the year 1219.
[4] Archdeacon of Totnes. He installed Serlo, the first Dean, 1225.
[5] One of this name was the Donor of some Vestments.—*Oliver's Lives*, p. 299.
[6] A martyrologium was compiled by order of Bishop Brantyngham.—See *Dugdale*, vol. ii., p. 518, Edit, 1819.

solent, qnedam tintinationes signorum qnasi ad adjutorium vocandum, quod tamen in aliis classicis nullo modo fit : ut sic habeatur eorum notitia et differentia—exceptis illis que primo fiunt pro Episcopis et Canonicis in ipso eorum obitu, ut supradictum est.

Quando nona pulsarii debet ante prandium et quando post prandium.[1]

Nota quod hora nona pulsatur quandoque ante prandium quandoque post prandium : post prandium vero pulsatur in die Pasche et cotidie, a die Pasche usque ad diem Sancti Michaelis nisi in diebus vigiliarum et jejuniorum tam ordinariorum quam extraordinariorum, et tunc pulsatur ante prandium. In die Sancti Michaelis et a die Sancti Michaelis usque ad diem cene, semper pulsatur psst missam ante prandium et in quadragesima omni enim die per quadragesiman exceptis solis dominicis pulsatur nona ante missam. In dominicis enim pulsatur post missam ut ante quadragesimam.

De pulsatione ad tertiam et modo pulsationis omnibus diebus per annum sive fiat processio sive non et precipue in qnadragesima.

Ad processionem pulsatur omni die dominica quando de dominica agitur post missam capituli, inter primam et tertiam et tunc non pulsatur aliter ad tertiam licet facta processione statim cantetur tertia. In omnibus aliis festis processiones habentibus post sonitum tertie dum cantatur tertia pulsatur ad processionem, et facta processione statim incipietur missa. In Letaniis autem et jejuniis pro aliqua necessitate in dictis, quibus processiones fiunt dum dicitur *Canon misse* solent fieri earum pulsationes. In ferialibus vero diebus quadragesime ad earum processiones semper pulsari debet post sonitum none dum ipsa cantatur.

---

[1] Formerly, each of the twenty-four Canons had his Priest Vicar, and it was thought highly desirable that they should reside near the Cathedral. With this view, Bishop Brantyngham in the year 1388 completed a public hall, private chambers, a kitchen, and other offices to enable them to live in community.—(*Reg.* vol. i. fol. 184.) We may conclude that the pulsation of the Bells before and after dinner was for these Priest-Vicars. See *Archæologica*, vol. xviii. p. 385. for the ancient constitutions of the Cathedral.

De modo pulsationis noctis Natalis Domini noctis Pasche et aliarum noctium tam in estate quam in yeme per totum annum et ignitegii.

In nocte Natalis Domini pulsandum est ad matutinas per duas horas ante mediam noctem. In omni duplici festo enim extra paschale tempus in media nocte et per estatem usque cap. Augusti. Semper pulsandum est in die Pasche ita mane ut si fieri potest, inter diem et noctem. Semper in crastino et per totam septimanam ut clarius sit dies per totum. Post septimanam Pasche usque ad festum Sancte Trinitatis ita diluculo surgatur ut dictis matutinis illuscescat dies. In festo Sancte Trinitatis ante solis occubitum ita pulsande sunt matutine, ut due nocturne possint expleri ante noctem. Similiter fiat in Nativitate Sancti Johannis. Et in passione Apostolorum Petri et Pauli, necnon in translatione Sancti Thomæ Martyris, et in festo Sancti Petri ad vincula. In aliis autem festis, et profestis secundum quod servicium exigerit, et noctium brevitas permiserit citius et citius surgendum est, usque ad festum Sancti Michaelis. Tunc enim et deinde parciende sunt noctes tali modo ut pulsetur ignitegium solito tardius secundum noctium accrescentiam ut post ignitegium[1] residuum noctis in duas partis dividiatur, in cujus ultima pulsandum est ad matutina nisi aliqua internalis festivitas obstet, cujus servicii prolixitas citius surgendum expectat.[2]

Bishop Oldham, in his *Statutes* 1511, directs how the Annualarii (or Chantry Priests) were to sound or toll a certain number of times with one bell, then a full tolling of all the bells at the canonical hours, after the accustomed manner; at the close of which the service was to begin.

The following extract is from Bishop Oldham's *Statutes*.

"De modo pulsandi ad Divina.

"Annuellariis*** ulterius precipimus quatinus solitas pulsaciones ad

[1] Curfew.
[2] See *Archæologia*, vol. xviii, p. 403, in a note from Tyrwhitt's *Chaucer*, vol. ii, p. 244, &c. "Not so called from receiving a yearly stipend, but from being employed solely in singing annuals or anniversary masses for the dead, without any cure of souls."

horas canonicas debita forma faciant. Proviso quod ad matutinas et ad vesperas in Feriis et Festis, cum Regimine Chori[1] vel sine tantomodo loco tempore pulsacionis quotidianæ faciant sexaginta aut plures Tintinaciones cum majori campana de tribus minoribus in Australi Turre dependentibus. Et simili modo in Festis principalibus et majoribus duplicibus, post terciam pulsacionem, dictas faciant Tintinaciones: quibus finitis sequatur statim completa pulsacio cum aliis campanis more solito pulsanda."

Surely very like to this is the present use. Every person living within sound of these glorious bells knows that at the hours of service each bell is first sounded a few times, and then the whole are sounded or chimed in succession; may it not, therefore, be fairly presumed that this has sprung from the ancient usage; and though it may have been interrupted in the days of anarchy and confusion, yet upon the return of better things, the old way would have been in remembrance of some and would be restored, serving for daily use, as Risdon tells us was the practice in his time.

In another section of his statutes, "De exhibitione cereorum," &c., we see the beginning of laymen being allowed to handle the bells.[2]

The next record to be noticed is dated 6 May, 1552 (6 Edw. VI.,) at which time a Commission was issued to take an Inventory of Church Goods within the City of Exeter. A copy of the return was found in the old Receiver's office, at the top of the Guildhall, by Mr. Stewart Moore of London, when employed upon the City Archives, and there the long-looked for Record of the Bells of the Cathedral was discovered in the form of a rough Draught and a fair copy. It is the more valuable as the original does not exist in the Augmentation Office. The articles of instruction will be found in the Appendix.

---

[1] This refers to the Rulers of Choirs in the middle ages, for an explanation of which see the Consuetudines of Sarum, in Dr. Roch's *Church of the Fathers*, also the *Servers' Hand Book, and the Services of the Church, with Rubrical Directions according to the use of Sarum*, by Charles Walker, Esq., published by Hayes and Palmer, London.

[2] Sec. 3: "In duplicibus autem festis maxime in majoribus custos, minister, cantor, et sacrista, quilibet eorum unum famulum fidelem ad pulsandum cum clericis in eorum adjutorium oportuerit transmittant vel cum eis faciant pernoctare."—(See Oliver's *Monasticon*, p. 272-3.)

Things reserved in the Cath. Chirch, and committed to the custodie of Mr. Treasourer & the Chapt^r there:

Inprimis ther tenne belles y^e in ij towers, y^t is to saie.

In ye one Tower.
- One great bell called Granndsons of xl^c waight by estimacon.
- Itm. Stafford's bell, of xx^c waight by estimacon.
- Itm. Trynitie bell, of xxvij^c waight by estimacon.
- Itm. Magdalene bell, of xxij^c waight by estimacon.
- Itm, (?) anoth. called Domme bell. of xxvi^c waight by estimacon.
- Itm. anoth. called Mary, of xvij^c weight by estimacon.
- Itm. anoth. of xix^c waight by estimacon.
- Itm. anoth. of x^c waight by estimacon.

In ye other Tower.
- Itm. ye clok bell of xxxiij^c by estimacon.
- Itm. anoth. of viij^c
- Itm. anoth. of vj^c
- Itm. anoth. of v^c
- Itm. anoth. of iiij^c
} by estimacon.

The whole waight of all ye said bells together is xxvij and six hundred waight by estimacion.

What the Commissioners at the view of the Cathedral Church goodes of Exon have found there.

viij belles in one toew^r namelie, y^{es} 1

Bishop Granndson's bell	...	1	XL^c
B Stafford's bell ...	...	2	XXX^c
Trynitie bell ...	...	3	XXVIj^c
Magdalene bell ...	...	4	XXVIj^c
Domme bell ...	...	5	XXvj^c
The sixte bell ...	...	6	xix^c
The major bell ...	...	7	XVIj^c
The eight ...	...	8	X^c

} waight by estimacon.

Suma xix^x and vi^x waight.

The above is considered to be a rough copy, or draft; it is on paper.

Item v belles remayning in anothʳ towʳ [1]

The first called yᵉ clock bell ...	1 ...	xxxvIIj	
The second	2 ...	vIIjᶜ	waight by estimacon.
The thirde	3 ...	vIᶜ	
The fourth	4 ...	vᶜ	
The fifth	5 ...	IIIjᶜ	

Summa tōlis of all yᵉ whole waight of yᵉ belles in the too towʳˢ } xxv thousand and seven hundreth waight.

Of yᵉˢ belles it is necessary yᵗ yᵉ great or Granndson's bell remayne to tolle to yᵉ sermon. itm. yᵉ clock bell, and one to ryng to dailie prayˢ˙

It appears by this last paragraph that under the sanction of the Bishop, to whom the Articles of Instruction were specially addressed by the Commission, all the bells in the Cathedral, but three, were to be removed! There must have been a delay, an unwillingness it is to be hoped, on the part of the Dean and Chapter, to carry out this recommendation; and as Edward VI. died a few months afterwards (6 July 1553) on the accession of Queen Mary, it may be supposed, things remained as they were; and so the bells were saved, and there they continued certainly till Risdon's time, who in his *Survey of Devon*, which is supposed to have been written before 1640, speaking of the number in the south tower, tells us "there be eight bells[1] serving for daily use, which were escheated with all the Church goods in the sixth year of Edward VI., by commission and commandment then given to the Treasurer of the Church, for answering the same at all demands."[2]

What Risdon means by saying "serving for daily use," I take, they were chimed for service something in the way they are now, and if so, the probability is, that the present mode of chiming, (I do not mean to say with the wooden keys or levers, and hammers striking outside the bells) has come down to us by tradition, and is a relic of the use practised in Bishop Quivil's time.

[1] Some of these were probably the work of Roger de Ropeford.
[2] No doubt the same bells which are enumerated in the Commission.

Though it appears from the date of the Bell Ringer's Office in 1676 (see Appendix iii) that even at that date chiming all the bells is not alluded to, but he is to toll the Oldham[1] bell a quarter of an hour after Nine o'clock in the morning, and a quarter after Three o'clock in the afternoon for Service in the quire.

In 1582, 25 July, 24 of Elizabeth. Agreement between the Dean and Chapter of Exeter and Hugh Chapindon of Southmolton.

Whereas the said Dean and Chapter have paid the said Hugh £20 "for and in full satisfaction of a cheime by him the sayed Hughe Chapingdon made in the southe tower of the sayd Cathed. Churche," the said Hugh agrees to keep it in order for two years, "and also shall at his like cost and charges cause the sayd cheime to strike and serve for all the bells of the sayd tower, if at anye tyme hearafter the sayd Deane and Chapter or theire successors shall newe caste or cause to be new caste or exchaunged suche of the sayd bells as be not tuneable at this present." Signed, "By me Hugh Chappyngton."

In the Acts of Chapter, 21 March, 1611, "Decreed as follows, that the Peter bell crazed 5 November last past should be new cast at the charge of the Church, the consideration and good husbandry of that business is referred to any four, three, or two of the Chapter that will meet this next week about the same."

In the same book, 13 April, 1612, they decreed as follows, "That according to a former Act made 21 of March last, the Peter bell should be new cast by Mr. John Birdall in the workhouse of the Church, or in Mr. Dean's yard, with such addition of metal as shall be convenient, the consideration whereof is to be had as in the present Act, 21 March last is contained."

Agreement with John Birdall.

By an entry in the Chapter Act Book (No. 3553, f 26), 6 June, 1612. A schedule of covenants was decreed between the Chapter and John

---

[1] No bell is now known by that name, but as it was tolled about 9 o'clock, it was probably the one now called "Old nine o'clock."

Birdall, bellfounder, concerning the new casting of Peter Bell, to be sealed with their common seal. And further they decreed a ringe of eight bells in the south tower to be made perfect and tuneable at the charge of the Deane and Chapter, to be performed by the said John Birdall upon such covenants as shall be agreed upon betweene them. And that a chyme be set upp in the said tower by John Savadge, according to an agreement already made betweene Mr. Treasurer, Mr. Archdeacon Helyar, and Mr. Bodley in the behalf of the Chapter and the said John Savadge.

If Birdall did cast the Peter according to the order of Chapter, it must have been crazed again, for the present date on that noble bell is 1676, when it was cast by Thomas Purdue.

The next entry in the *Act Book* is 6 April, 1616—"They decreed that John Birdall should new cast and make tuneable the bells in the south tower, and to be allowed for his charge the sum of thirty-eight pounds six shillings and eightpence according to the schedule of covenants contained in paper and now read in the Chapter, and that the said covenants be engrossed and one part of them sealed with the Chapter seal." His initials (Fig. 1) are found on the present second bell, dated 1616, with the intermediate stamp, Fig. 2.

Fig. 1.   Fig. 2.

Act Book, 3553, f. 69, 16 July, 1617. They decreed that John Eglon should make a new wheele for Stafford Bell, and (upon triall of his sufficiencie for the same, and reasonablcness in the price) to goe onward wth the rest of the wheeles, if the Chapter shall so thinke fit.

24 July, 1624. They decreed the new casting of Peter Bell to the care of Mr. Archdeacon Helyar.

The next entry in the *Act Book* dated 29 April, 1625, decreed that three bells in the South Tower, viz., "Grandison bell, Nine o'clock bell, and the third thick bell of the ring be new cast by Mr. Pennington, who is to have for his labour for all manner of charges belonging to the same, forty pounds, and entering into covenants and giving his voluntary oath of the true performance of the said work."

There is no bell of the date of that Act, and nothing was probably done, as there is a similar order in *Act Book*, 5 September, 1629, when it was "decreed that Mr. Pennington do cast the three bells, viz., Grandison, the Nine o'clock bell, and the third bell in the South Tower, and to free the Chapter by covenant of all manner of charges belonging to the same whatsoever, and to have for his labour upon finishing that work fifty pounds.

There are no bells of that date—the nearest is the 4th. (A flat, called *Pongamouth*) which was cast by Thomas Pennington of Exon, 1630.

FRIEZE ORNAMENT USED BY PENNINGTON. Fig. 3.

The next bell, according to date, is the 3rd re-cast by John Pennington in 1658; and then we come to 1676, the date on the 4th

(A natural); the 7th, called *Cobthorne* (from the Dean of that name, elected 1419); the 9th, called *Stafford* (Bishop, 1395 to 1419); and *Great Peter*, the whole of which were re-cast by Thomas Purdue.

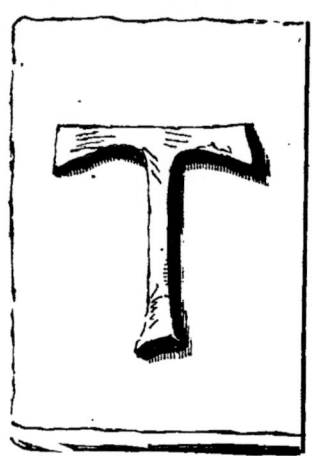 

PURDUE'S INITIALS.

The next record shows what became of "the four broken bells in the north tower," mentioned above.

26 May, 1676. The Dean and Chapter of St. Peter's, Exeter, and Thomas Purdue of Closworth (Somerset), Belfounder, and Thomas Heart of Long Sutton (Somerset), Carpenter.

"Copy. Articles of agreement for the recasting and rehanging of those four bells following now hanging and being in the Cathedral Church of S. Peter aforesaid: that is to say, the bell called Peter bell, the bell called Grandison, the bell called Stafford, and the tenor or greate bell of the small ring, being all att present crazed; which bells are to bee new cast, and to bee as bigg as they were, and valuable, tuneable, and musical, and to agree in tune and musicke with the other bells of the said Church, whereof Richard Beavis, Esq. or any person or persons well skilled in such matters is or are to be judges."[1]

By the Act' Book it appears that Purdue and Heart are to take down and rehang ready for ringing by 25 December for £260, and £20 more if Richard Beavis shall award that Purdue deserves it, which he did, and his Cobthorne bell, which was not perfect, so he enters into a bond 27 Feb. 1676, in £100 if it fails within twenty years.

"And whereas since the new castinge the said bells one of the said four bells, to wit, the said bell commonly called THE Tenor or Great Bell of the small ring, or Cobthorne bell, appeareth to bee defective in the HEAD, PALLAT, and CANONS or tenons thereof, and to be baser mettle in those parts than in the other parts thereof and than any the other bells of that tower, insoemuch that the said Cobthorne bell cannot be hung up by the canons or tenons and argent thereof, as the same was formerly, and still ought to bee hung and as other bells are usually hung, but is at present hung up by iron bolts, for and in the doeing which the said Thomas Purdue hath caused to bee made and bored diverse holes through the head or pallat of the said bell:" if therefore the said bell become defective within twenty years the said Thomas Purdue will recast it.—

   Signed,   "Thomas [T. P.] Purdue."[1]

1676. *Monies issued forth towards casting of the Bells.*

	£	s.	d.
Impri. delivered Canon Neighbour for the erecting of a house	12	0	0
Item paid the Bellfounder 7ʰ· Julii, 1676, ut per note	40	0	0
Item pᵈ· the men for drawing up Peter Bell		6	0
It. pᵈ· the Bellfounder 17 Aug. ut patet per a quitt	30	0	0
Pᵈ· for weighing Peter Bell and Cobthorne		9	6
Pᵈ· 25 Sept. to Tho. Hart by order of Dr. Copplestone and George Nayls, ordered	20	0	0
Pᵈ· 13 Oct. '76, to Tho. Purdew by order of Dr. Coppleston and Mr. D.	50	0	0
Pᵈ· for weighing Grandison and Stafford		7	9
Pᵈ· 15 Dec. '76, to Mr. Purdew	60	0	0
Pᵈ· Mr. Lousemore for weighing Cobthorne		2	0

[1] There the bell still hangs by the bolts, sound and good with the exception of the canons as it came out of the mould, 1676.

PURDUE'S BORDER ON THE COBTHORNE, GRANDISSON, AND GREAT PETER. Fig. 4.

Item paid 12 Jan. to Tho. Hart	5	0	0
Item p^d. Mr. Loosemore, Hart the bellfounders' bill dat. 19, for mending the old bells	2	6	0
Item to Tho. Hart, by Order	20	0	0
It. p^d. 23 Feb. '76, to Tho. Hart in full of the articles betw. the Chapter and himself	30	0	0
Item p^d. 27 Feb. to Tho. Purdew	120	0	0
Item p^d. 28 Feb. to Tho. Purdew	40	0	0
Item p^d. 23 Marcii to Tho. Purdew in further parte of the new bell	5	0	0
Item p^d. Mr. Loosemore, Harts the Carp^rs. bill for hanging the new bell	4	0	0
Item p^d. Mr. Loosemore, Dowdall the Carp^rs. bill dat. 21 Feb., '76, for his work about the Clapper	6	0	0

—From Fabric Accounts on the Fly Leaf. Vol. No. 3776

1678 *Bells on the Sally. Chapter Accounts.*[1]

Item p^d. Mr. Warren towards the hanging the bells to be rung upon the Sally	20	0	0
Item p^d. more to Mr. Warren towards the hanging of the bells Sally-way	20	0	0
Item paid Mr. Warren, Bellfounder, in full of agreement to put the bells Sally-way	20	0	0

The next entry in the Chapter Acts is dated 28 September, 1689:

"Upon report that Mr. Beavis hath made a bargain with the bell-founder to re-cast the bell[2] for twenty pounds, they did agree to the said bargain, and that the bell be taken down and put up at the charge of the bell-founder, who is to have three pounds more in case Mr. Beavis approves of the bell when new cast."

[1] This upsets the tradition that the Bells were so hung by Bilbie in 1778.
[2] Which of the bells cannot be found.

There is no bell of that date—but the order for re-casting the *Doom* bell dated 1693, appears in the *Act Book*, 24 September, 1692, "Ordered the bell commonly called the *Doom Bell*, lately cast by Mr. Pennington, to be new cast by Mr. Thomas Purdue, of Closworth, Somerset, bell-founder, and to be made tuneable and useful in his place, and that Thomas Purdue be contracted with for the same, as Mr. Beavis shall direct for the new casting of the same, and making the said bell full weight, the sum to be contracted for not exceeding twenty pounds, besides allowance for metal to be added."

1691 Paid to and for account of the Bellfounder (Pennington) severall times and by severall orders -   16 0 6

1693 Paid to Thomas Purdue and Thomas Knight, Bell-founders, for new casting the Doome Bell, and adding 583$^{lbs.}$ and ½ of Mettle thereto, as per note allowed by Mr. Beavis and Mr. Treasurer according to the articles -   - -   -   49 3 0

We now come to 1729, the date on the *Treble* or 1st; the 5th called *Fox* (after Bishop, from 1487 to 1491), the 8th *(old nine o'clock* re-cast before in 1629) and the 10th or *Grandison* (Bishop from 1327 to 1369), also re-cast before by Pennington in 1629; which were all re-cast by William Evans of Chepstow.

The order as entered in *Act Book*, 11 January, 1728-9, viz., "That the three bells which are new cracked be new cast with all convenient speed by some skilful hands, and that the others be new hung, in such manner as shall be adjudged proper, and that the president of the Chapter for the time being, and the residentiarys now present, or any two of them, be authorized to treat and contract with Mr. Evans, or any other skilful bell founder for the performance of this work."

The proposals made by Mr. Wm. Evans for doing the work, namely— "for recasting ye 3 crack'd bells of S. Peters, Exon, viz., ye 5th, 8th, and tenour, and likewise ye 3rd and 4th, tho' sound, this being necessary to make a complete musical peal of ten."

He sums up his proposals thus. The whole charge thus completed.—

For recasting 15,100lb. of metal at £1 8s 0d p^r. hund^d. ...	211	8	0
Taking ye bells down and hanging y^m up again ...	70	0	0
The allowance of 5lb. per hundred for waste to be supplied wth new metal at 1s. 2d p^r. p^d.	44	0	0
Six hundred p^d encrease of gross weight at 1s 2d p^r p^d ...	39	4	0
To ye Foundery	20	0	0
To ye Stocks	5	0	0
To y^e Workmen	2	2	0
	£391	14	0

By looking at the dates on the bells it will be seen that the above proposals as to the 3rd and 4th were not carried out, for they are dated 1658 and 1676, but four bells were recast by him, and not three.

INITIALS OF WILLIAM EVANS.

Looking at the various dates of the several bells which compose this noble ring, (surpassed by none in the kingdom, either in weight of metal, or richness of tone,) it is a matter of surprise that they harmonize so perfectly together. And, so scientifically has the whole ring been constructed, that, besides the ring of ten in B flat, of eight in B flat, of six in B flat, and six in F, which it contains, it is capable of producing (by the introduction of A flat,) three other rings, viz., one of six in E flat,[6] one of eight in C minor, and one of six in C minor. The capabilities of these bells are here set down in musical notes.

E

FIVE MAJOR.

TWO MINOR.

It is still a mystery *how* this noble ring was augmented from 8 to 10. The usual way would be to add two trebles, but that was not done, because the first is a "*recast*" dated 1729, and the second is dated 1616.

We are also ignorant when this noble peal was augmented from eight to ten. It was not done in 1729 by Evans, as might at first be supposed from the wording of his proposals just quoted.

In 1697, the date of Prince's Epistle dedicatory of his *Worthies of Devon*, at p. 166, in his remarks on Peter Courtenay, Bishop of Exeter, he says, "In the south tower is a cage of ten very sweet and musical bells." From these two dates it may be safely inferred that the ring or peal was made ten in 1676 when the Chapter agreed with Purdue to do the work recited in the foregoing extracts.

It appears in an entry in the ACT BOOK, dated 13 January, 1778, that Mr. Thomas Bilbie, Bellfounder (he lived at Cullompton) had delivered written proposals for new hanging and doing all other necessary repairs to the bells, putting the same into complete order, and he agreed to perform the same in a proper and workmanlike manner for the sum of forty guineas. He was to keep the said work in repair for one year from Michaelmas next, by which time the work was to be completed. His proposals were accepted and the work was done.

By tradition the work was done by one *Searle*, Bilbie's bellhanger—after which they were rung for the first time by fifteen men from Alphington, where, a few years before, a new ring of eight had been set up by Bilbie, and for many years afterwards the ringers from the same place continued to handle the bells.

Risdon, in his *Survey of Devon*, which is said to have been written before 1640, says, "There be eight bells serving for daily use, which were escheated in the sixth year Edward VI."

Judging from appearances nothing has been thoroughly done to them from that time to the present, excepting trifling mendings as occasion might require, and therefore it is not to be wondered at that they are not in that excellent order, which is so necessary for ringing, properly so called, that is half pull changes, indeed the tenors are too heavy for such use.

I must not close without a few words about *Great Peter* in the north tower, originally given by Bishop Courtenay in 1484.

On certain occasions that bell used to be rung, and it appears by entries in Acts of Chapter March 11th, 1611, quoted above, that it was crazed when rung on the 5th of November, 1610, and the present bell is a recast.

Godwin in his *Præsulibus*, fol. p. 234, under Bishop Courtenay, tells us that he presented the north tower with a very large bell "quæ propter pondus immensum sine multorum hominum labore non potest pulsari eamque ob causam duplicem habet rotam funesque binas quarum ope circum-agatur."

Brice in his *Dictionary*, under Exeter, published 1759, says it "used to be rung out on proper occasions, though it has not been rung out for many years past."

At present there are no wheels attached to this bell, and the curfew and other tollings are pulsed by means of a heavy hammer striking on the outside, and in this way it is tolled every morning for mattins fifteen minutes and then doubled ten minutes, after which the ringer walks away to the south tower and rings out the treble of the ten for five minutes till *Peter* strikes the hour. The curfew is tolled every evening after the clock strikes eight; the number of blows is regulated by the number of the days in the month, and after a pause eight blows are struck.

For the other services the following is the use; the sixth bell is struck four blows a minute for five minutes, and after that it is struck quickly for one minute, then the 7th, 8th, 9th, and 10th, each in succession one minute, after which the whole ten are pulsed in succession or chimed five minutes till *Peter* strikes the hour; which seems to be in accordance with the extract from Bishop Oldham's Statutes.

HEAD OF ARCHBISHOP LAUD ON THE GRANDISON BELL:

See Evelyn on Medals, fo., 1696, p. 114.

The Legends on the Cathedral Bells.

In the South Tower.

No.	Inscription	Name	Diam. Inches.	Thickness of Sound Bow. Inches.	Note.	Reputed Weight. cwt. qrs. lbs.
1	W. ⚜ E. RECAST, 1729	..	33¼	2¼	D	8 3 20
2	(2) **Anno Dō.** 1616 ▽ **E.B.** (See Figs. 1 and 2)	..	36	2⅜	C	9 3 12
3	IOHN o PENNINGTON o OF o EXON o NEW o CAST o ME o ANNO o DOMINI o 1658 .. (Coins stamped in 'us stops.)	..	37½	2⅞	B Flat.	10 1 12
4	THO.∴ PERDVE ∴ ME ∴ FECIT ∴ ANNO ∴ DOMINI ∴ 1676 ∴ EX ∴ IMPENSIS ∴ DECANI ∴ ET ∴ CAPITVLI ∴ EXON ∴	..	40½	3	A	12 2 0 11·0·18
4	RENOVAT : EX : IMPENSIS : DECANI : ET : CAPITOLI : EXON : THO. PENNINGTON : NEW : CAST : ME… ANNO : DOMINI : 1630 (A frieze of fleur-de-lis. Fig. 3) This bell not used with the Ten.	Pongamouth	41	3	A Flat.	11 (18) 30 11·0·18
5	W. ⚜ E. RECAST, 1729	Fox	46	3½	G	15 0 20 15·0·6
6	RENOVAT : EX : IMPENSIS : DECANI : ET : CAPITOLI : EXON : ANNO : DOMINI : 1693 : T. P. (Frieze of fleur-de-lis. Fig. 3)	Doom Bell	49	3½	F	20 3 26
7	EX : DONO : IOHANNIS : COBTHORNI : QUONDAM : DEC-ANI : EXON : TH. PVRDVE : FECIT : RENOVAT : EX : IMPENSIS : DECANI : ET : CAPITVLI : EXON : ANNO : DOMINI : 1676 .. (Star stops between all the words with mediæval borders of flowers. Fig. 4)	Cobthorne	55	4⅛	E Flat.	30 1 12

Total weight of 11 bells 266 cwts.

8	WILLIAM EVANS FECIT. RECAST 1729	Old 9 o'clock	59	4¼	D	38 1 16 ✓
9	EX : DONO : EDMVNDI : STAFFORD : EPISCOPI : EXON : PER : THO. : PERDVE : RENOVAT : EX : IMPENSIS : DECANI : ET : CAPITVLI : EXON : ANNO : DOM. : 1676 (Star stops ; mediæval border above and below. Fig. 4)	Stafford	64¼	4¼	C	40 3 14
10	EX DONO JOHANNIS GRANDISON o EPISCOPI EXON. GVLIEL EVANS FECIT 1729 (A medallion of Laud.) Recast 1902	Grandison	71½	4⅞	B Flat	67 1 18

new peal 7 bells augmented to 8 with fitting all 11 1910

The bells are not in good order; the bell-chamber is very clean and very conveniently furnished with ladders. The bells are hung so high that you may safely walk under them. They all swing one way. The 2nd, 4th, and 9th are maiden bells; all the others are more or less chipped inside, the 4th and 7th have no cannons.

In the North Tower.

	EX o DONO o PETRI o COVRTENAY o EPISCOPI o EXON ANNO DOM. : 1484 o PLEBS : PATRIÆ : PLAVDIT DUM : PETRVM : PLE o RENOVAT : EX : IMPENSIS : DECANI : ET : CAPITVLI : EXON : ANNO : DOMINI : 1676 o PER : THO. : PVRDVE o (The Clock Bell.) Mediæval frieze above and below. PLE is the end, intended for PLENIUS AUDIT. Coins are impressed between many words.	Great Peter	76	5	A	125 0 0

APPENDIX I.

In a book, small 4to, belonging to the Treasurer of the Cathedral, in which are copies of the Statutes of the Cathedral, drawn up 1670 by Baldwin Acland, Treasurer, there is the following entry :—

The fees and benefitt belonging to the Belringer.

"Imprs. Hee hath a chamber and lodgings over the north porch where Josias More lives.

Hee hath alsoe sometyme the fees and benefitt of the seates in the body of the Church.

He hath for keeping and attending the clock and bells from the Dean and Chapter, paid every quarter	16	2	2
For tolling the bell for every sick person		1	0
For every childe			6
For making every grave in the Cathedral, Cloyster, or Iles		3	4
For tolling the bell at every ffunerall Sermon		2	6
For opening the great doore at every ffunerall		1	6
For tolling a bell before Sermon at Easter Eve		2	6
For every buriall in any Church within the City and in St. Edmonds on the Bridge		2	6
For every one that is chested[1] in St. Peter's Churchyard, being a stranger sometimes iijs iiijd, or as they can agree		3	4
For all citizens of the younger sort chested and buryed in the Churchyard		1	0
For every persons buryall unchested			6
For buryall of every prisoner from the common goale			6
For every tombe or monument erected in the Churchyard, besides the Treasurer's fees		3	4

---

[1] By this expression one may suppose it was not uncommon to bury the dead without a coffin.

Besides he hath some benefitt for every tyme they ring for their pleasure with the leave of the Treasurer. And for shewing the 2 towers and bells to strangers.

And some benefitt heretofore from the garden within the Cloysters, and from ye City for tolling ye bell at eight o'clock.

The Bellringers office which is given by the Treasurer.

Hee is every morning at five of ye clock to toll and give warning according to ye custome.

Hee is to toll the bell again at six a clock every morning halfe an hower together for prayers and sermon.

Hee is to toll the Oldham bell a quarter of an hower after nine a clock in ye morning and a quarter after three a clock in the afternoon for service in ye Quire.

Hee is also to toll ye Sermon bell every Sunday after the 2nd lesson of the Quire Service in ye morning when there is a sermon, and every night at eight of the Clock.

Hee is to keep and attend ye Clock diligently.

He is to keep the bells in good order and to provide ropes when there is need at ye charge of the Deane and Chapter and the Treasurer.

These are the fees, and this is ye duty and office of the Bellringer according to ye orders and customes of the Cathedral Church of St. Peter in Exeter, as I find them recorded and testifyed by credible witnesses.

Signed, April 21, 1670.   BALDWIN ACLAND."

In an after memorandum, date 15 February, 1676:—

"These forementioned papers concerning the office and ffees of the Virgers and Bellringers are true copeyes taken out of Treasurer Robert Hall's papers.
    Examined by us,
                    NICH. HALL, Treasurer.
                    RICHD. DYMOND."

My thanks are due to the present Treasurer for the above extracts.

APPENDIX II.

The following is an account of the Records of the Cathedral bells discovered among the archives of the Exeter Corporation by Mr. Stewart Moore, as published in the *Exeter Gazette*, 3 January, 1868.

It appears from an old volume of memoranda in the possession of the Corporatiou that a Special Commission was issued 16 May, 6 Edward VI. (1552), addressed to Myles, Bishop of Exeter, Sir Thomas Denys, Knight, the then Mayor of Exeter, Sir Peter Carew, Knight, and Richard Chydley, Thomas Prestwode, and John Mydwynter, Esquires. It recites that, "Whereas we have att sondrye times heretofore by our Specyall Commyssion and otherwise commanded that ther shuld be taken and made a juste viewe survey and Invintorie of all manner of goodes, plate, jewles, vestyments, bells, and other ornaments within every parishe belongyng or in any wyse appertaynyng to any Churche, chapell, brothered, gylde, or fraternyte wt'in thys our Realme of England," and that such goodes so inventoried should be given into safe custody and be ready to be produced at all times. This was accordingly done, and the inventories thereof were made by indenture, one part remaining with the Custos Rotulorum of the county or his deputy, and the other part with the churchwardens or those who had charge of the said goods. "And other inventories also made by oure commandment by oure bysshopes and ther ecclesyastycal officers were lekewyse by them retorned hether to oure Councell." "Yet nevertheless for that we be informed that some parte of the same goods, plate, jewelles, belles, and ornaments of Churches be in some places imbesyled or removed contrarye to our former expresse commandments and manyfestly to the contempte and derogacion of our honour in that behalf," we have appointed you to take a full and just view of all goods, &c., in whose hands soever they be within the county of the city of Exeter, and upon such view to make a full inventory and to compare it ormer inventories remaining with the churchwardens, &c.; to inquire concerning the defaults in such goods, &c., according to the tenor of certain articles of instruction which accompany the Commission.

The Commission also gives power to punish any persons who refuse to obey the Commissioners in the execution of it.

The Articles of Instruction are as follows :—

I. The Commissioners to assemble immediately on receipt of the Commission.

II. To command the Custos Rotulorum or the Clerk of the Peace to deliver to them "such bokes registers and Invyntories as hath heretofore any wyse come to their hands by Indenture, touching the sommes numbers and valewes of any goodes plate jewells vestements bells," and likewise to the Bishop of the Diocese and his officers, &c. To receive the said Inventories, and "accordyng to the best rechest and grettyst Invintorie the sayd Commyssioners shall procede to make their survey and inquyre and by the same make the searches of the defaultes and wantes that shall be founde," and not only by the "viewe of the said Registers and Invintories but also by any other means they can better devyse procede to the due searche and inquisition of the wantes and defaultes of any parte of the said goodes, plate, jewles, vestements, belles, or ornaments."

III. To obtain the Inventories more speedily the Commissioners shall receive special letters of commandment to be used as they see occasion.

IV. The Commissioners to cause to be made "Bills or books indented" of all goods, &c. "as yet be remayning or anywyse fourthcomying." One part to be returned to the Privy Council, the other to remain with those who have charge of the said goods, &c. "And they schall also geve good charge and order that the seme goodes and every parte thereof be at altymes ffourthcomying to be answered; leyving never the lasse in everye parishe churche or chappell of comen resorte one, too, or more chalyces or cuppys accordying to the multitude of the people in every suche churche and chappell, and also suche ornamentes as by ther dyscression may seme requysette for the devyne service in every suche place for the tyme."

V. "Because we are informed that in many places great quantities of the said plate, jewels, belles, and ornaments be imbeseled by certyn private men contrary to oure expresse commandements in that behalf," the Commissioners are "substancyously and justly to enquere and attayne the knowledge therof by whos faulte the same ys and hath been, and in whos handes any parte of the same is come," &c., &c.

VI. "Apon a full serche and inquyre wherof" the Commissioners are to call before them all persons by whom the said plate, jewels, &c., have been "alienated, imbesiled, or taken away," and to do their best to recover the same, certifying to the Privy Council the names of all who refuse to obey their order touching the re-delivery of the same.

VII. "Fynally oure pleasure ys that the said Commyssioners in all there doynges shall use suche sober and dyscrete maner of prossidying as the effecte of thys commission may go fforward with as myche quyet and as lytell occasion of troble or disquyett of the multytude as may be, usying to that ende suche wyse perswaysing in all places of there sessions as in respecte of the place and dysposission of the people may seme to there wysedom moste expedyent, gevying also good and substanciall order for the staye of thenordynate and greedy covytuoussnese of such dysordered people as have or shall go aboute the alienatyng of any of the premysses so as accordyng to reason and order suche as have or shall contemptuysly offend in thys behalffe may receve reformacion as for the qualytie of their doynges shall be requysette."

This last paragraph would seem to show that the Commission was looked upon with little favour by the people generally.

These records were found in a box with many other papers, wormeaten to the last degree, and much injured by damp ; indeed, the box was so much decayed that the bottom of it fell to powder. Fortunately, nearly all the inventories have been recovered, and only a few are badly injured. There are, however, duplicates of many of them, and a perfect set exists for all the parishes in the city. They are more particularly valuable because the duplicates of the greater part of them, including that of the Cathedral, which ought to exist in the Public Record Office in London, are missing.

APPENDIX III.

Bell Metall appropriated.

7 October 1615. Robert Lane, Treasurer of the Cathedral, Thomas Barret and William Helyar, Canons Residentiary now stewards there, to the Archbishop of Canterbury and other, his Majesty's Commission for causes ecclesiastical.

Petition—Praying that one John Sprott, Canon Residentiary, should be compelled to pay for or return to the Dean and Chapter 1700[lb] of bell metal sold away by him as he had been ordered; but he had not done so, to the detriment of the Church and hinderance for the newe casting of certen old bells there.

It is further prayed that the money so to arise, may be employed towards the newe casting and making tuneable eight other bells there nowe imperfect, and settying up a chyme as by this Court alredy hathe beene ordered. And also towards the making and setting upp of a watch diall on the outside of the north tower of that Church wth bells and quarter-strikers, as it is at Westminster, w[ch] will be very useful to the whole cittye and many others that passe that way, being a great thoroughfare.

Further, they pray that Mr. Sprott be compelled to make satisfaction in money, for the bell metal sold was worth above £57; and these petitioners doe veryly beleve that £20 more at least will not procure so much mettall and so good as that w[ch] was solde.

Sprott. 25 *February*, 1614-15.

They decreed that the Chapter Clerk doe write a coppie of the order made 9th Februarii, 1614, by the Archbishop of Canterbury and other of his Maj[ties] Commissioner for causes ecclesiasticall, touching certain

Bell mettal heretofore sold and nowe to be bought in againe for uses in the said order expressed; and to include the said coppie in a letter and to direct it unto Mr. John Sprott, Sub-deane, and to delyver the same letter unto Mr. Tröt, his Vicar, to be with all speed accordingly conveyed, that the said Mr. Sprott may thereby take notice of so much of that order as by him is to be performed.—*Chapter Act Book, No. 3553, f. 49b.*

25 *March*, 1615.

Item. Mr. Treasurer, Mr. Barret, and Mr. Helyar desired securitye to be given to the said Dean and Chapter touching the bell mettall, according to an order made in that behalf by his Maj[ties] High Commissioners and read this day in the Chapter. Whereupon Mr. Deane offered to give securitye directly or indirectly as the Deane and Chapter shall think convenient. Mr. Sub-deane affirmed that he had given securitye alreadye, the said Mr. Treasurer, Mr. Barret, Mr. Helyar affirming that they had no such securitye, and still desiring the same might be given in the Chapter.—*Chapter Act Book, No. 3553, fol. 50.*

13 *January*, 1615.

Upon showing of an order made by his Ma[ties] High Commissioners by Mr. Sprott, Sub-deane, touching the fiftie seaven pounds remayning in the Receavers hands for bell mettall, they decreed presentlye upon Mr. Deanes returne from London to imploy the said money according to the said order.—*Chapter Act Book, No. 3553, f. 57b.*

Printed by Libri Plureos GmbH in Hamburg, Germany